THEY LONG TO END DEMOCRACY:

THE OLIGARCHY

SCOTT ROBINSON

Copyright ©2024 by Paleos Media

ISBN 979-8303636026

Author photograph by Josh Robinson

Cover art: 100 Covers

Note

The descriptive THE NATURE OF OLIGARCHY section of the book contains most of the content from the shorter book *What the Hell is the Oligarchy?*, by the author.

Some content in "Oligarchy: The Reagan Revolution" first appeared in *Red Brains, Blue Brains: The Psychology of MAGA*, by the author.

They Long to End Democracy

The GOP
Christian Nationalism
The Oligarchy
They Long to End Democracy (omnibus)

The *What the Hell is?* series...

Neoliberalism
Oligarchy
Christian Nationalism
Authoritarianism
Project 2025

STAND: A Handbook for Resisting Authoritarianism
Star Trek and Humanism
To Everything That Might Have Been
So Far from Tribe and Fire

Table of Contents

Series Preface:
They Long to End Democracy

"Welcome to the end of democracy!" cried conservative activist Jack Posobiec at the Conservative Political Action Conference in February 2024. "We are here to overthrow it completely."

This isn't a fringe group; this isn't an extremist rant. This is word from on high from the mainstream GOP.

That's not to say that Posobiec himself isn't a fringe extremist; he was, in fact, the biggest proponent of the Pizzagate conspiracy. But at CPAC, he was speaking for conservatives across the spectrum.

"We didn't get all the way there on January 6," he went on, almost indifferent to the breathtaking brazenness of confessing affinity with the insurrectionists who assaulted the US Capitol, "but we will endeavor to get rid of it and replace it with this, right here," he continued, gesturing to his audience and then raising his fist.

This is astonishing, something we never thought we'd hear proclaimed so candidly and publicly. But it is a fact, and has been for decades, that there are sizeable groups in the US that not only long for the ending of democracy in America, but have organized and labored to bring it about. And these aren't speculations: three groups have been very frank about it.

I can't speak for the Millennials or the Zoomers, but I can speak for my own generation, I think: in the

Boomer's America, the nation's status as the world's first true and oldest surviving democracy is truly a shiny gleaming point of pride. We're pretty darned thrilled to live in a democracy, a template of government that is so awesome and prestigious that it's been endlessly copied throughout the Western world over the past dozen decades or so. Go USA!

I'll also take the position that us Boomers – and the Gen Xers, too, I think – can lay claim to a more sober and nuanced appreciation of the Land of the Free than our elders or our kids. The Silents – not just my parents, but my teachers, dentists, and camp counselors – were utterly gung-ho over it, having grown up watching all of democracy's inglorious alternatives hovering like sinister buzzards at the edge of both oceans. And the Millennials and Zoomers are, au contraire, jaded to the gills about democracy, having watched the buzzards circle above them right here at home, from birth.

Me and mine, we got lots of both – democracy victorious, democracy getting its ass kicked. We watched Saigon fall, then watched the Berlin Wall do the same; we watched our government self-police by pushing out an odious chief executive, then watched it jump on another chief executive's warmongering Middle East bandwagon. We witnessed the Supreme Court's blessing of corporation personhood, saw *Shakespeare in Love* take *Saving Private Ryan*'s Oscar, watched Jethro Tull win a Best Album Grammy.

The impossible-to-deny truth of the matter is that the spectrum of sentiment we see around us, where democracy is concerned, is well-earned: no doubt about it, democracy is messy. Inconvenient. At times, downright stressful. And that's exactly what we sign up for, like going to an Eighties rock nostalgia festival and sitting through Skid Row and Slayer to get to Bon Jovi and Def Leppard.

Beyond our scale of enthusiasm for democracy, however, is an entirely different class of American: those who not only find it messy and inconvenient, but want it *done away with altogether*. Gone. Kaput. Outta here. And not just some fringe-y wingnuts: *tens of millions* of Americans feel this way.

And they feel strongly enough to act on it. Or, more precisely, they feel strongly enough that they're willing to go along with those who are acting it.

They fall into three distinct (albeit overlapping) groups, each of which will get a spotlight in this brief series.

The GOP

The GOP and US conservatives are not explicitly the same thing, but since the Gingrich Revolution in Congress, GOP non-conservatives have been quietly (and sometimes not-so-quietly) shown the door; GOP moderates are all but gone completely, and the left-leaning Republican has gone the way of the dodo bird. The GOP's obsession with conservative purity has stripped it of all diversity of thought and worldview, and the remainder has focused, for three decades now, on achieving "one-party rule".

Tom DeLay and Dick Armey succeeded Gingrich in party leadership on a platform of exactly that, laboring diligently – but only partially effectively – to shut out any and all bipartisan Congressional initiatives, leaving us with a GOP that now condemns and ousts its own whenever they dare to reach across the aisle.

It's not just Democrats who are the enemy; it's democracy itself. The GOP, its leadership, its Congressional caucus, its judges and justices, have all given the nod to a brazenly authoritarian presidential nominee who has stated in unambiguous terms that he intends to dismantle checks and balances and impose a dictatorial rule.

Christian Nationalists

The GOP's staunch allies in this quest are Evangelical Christians, who likewise long for the end of democracy in favor of the imposition of a Christian government, which they insist was the Founders' original intent.

This idea has been in the water supply of the Christian Right for decades as well, and was the impetus behind its alliance with the political right in the Eighties. The idea that America is a "Christian" nation and should be governed by Christians is a long-standing one, now a defining motivation in conservative politics.

And the GOP has been happy to take full advantage of it. "All glory is not to government," said Posobiec in his CPAC speech, "All glory to God."

Less public is the Society for American Civic Renewal, a secret, men-only society of wealthy white leaders who plan to restore white male domination in the US, implementing their version of Christianity in its government through a "regime change", according to reporting by Josh Kovensky of Talking Points Memo.

SACR's integration of Christian nationalism with its planned right-wing governance was laid bare, Kovensky wrote, in a speech by SACR member Russ Vought, who explained his vision for a US border policy that unites that nationalism with conservative aversion to pluralism by modeling that policy on Old Testament law, allowing in only those immigrants that "accept Israel's God, laws, and understanding of history."

The Christian nationalist movement's leadership has stoked the movement's base by instilling a fearful defensiveness, convincing them that "secularists" and "socialists" are out to eliminate religion in American society and marginalize them completely – which isn't true, but they readily accept it and act on it. They want a Christian government in part because they want their own worldview and beliefs to prevail over others, but also in part to protect them from their perceived enemies.

Ideologically, this Christian nationalist desire for control is called dominionism, explicitly declaring that Christians should take moral, spiritual, and ecclesiastical control of American society – and the way to do this is by taking over the government. Many extreme right-wing politicians – Ted Cruz, for example – are Christian dominionists.

The Oligarchy

"Oligarchy is rule of, by, and for the rich," writes Thom Hartmann in his handbook on the subject. "Oligarchs have unsuccessfully tried, twice, to replace democracy in America with oligarchy. Today, they are nearly finished with not only attempting a third time to change the American experiment from a democracy to Democracy is rule of, by, and for the people; oligarchy is rule of, by, and for the rich. This book details how oligarchs have unsuccessfully tried, twice, to replace democracy in America with oligarchy. Today, they are nearly finished with not only attempting a third time to change the American experiment from a democracy to oligarchs—rise up through seemingly democratic processes and take complete or near-complete control of government. From there, oligarchs typically begin to, as Steve Bannon said was the main goal of the Trump administration, "deconstruct the administrative state," seizing control over and corrupting every subordinate agency of government, from those responsible for enforcing the laws and the courts, to regulatory agencies, to those controlling the nation's currency and economy.

"We are living through America's third struggle with oligarchy. It began in 1971, when Lewis Powell, himself a proud agent of the tobacco oligarchs, laid out in a famous memo to the US Chamber of Commerce a plan for the various oligarchs of America to stop competing and organize to take over the US government. By 1980, the plan was in full flower, and by the late 1990s, the oligarchs directly or indirectly controlled a majority of the states, the entire Republican Party, and, at the federal level, well over half of the Democratic Party. By 2005, oligarchic control over the executive branch of our federal government was largely in place, and it was cemented with the Trump administration. When Donald Trump - himself an oligarch - came to power in January 2017, he and his agents embarked on a campaign to destroy the institutions of America that had been so carefully built up over more than 240 years. They succeeded in damaging and corrupting every single federal regulatory agency and turned the foundational departments within the executive branch into full-fledged agents of the Trump oligarchy."

For years now, the most prominent US oligarch has been Charles Koch, who had very publicly supported politicians who promote his libertarian cause and invested hundreds of millions in cultivating grass roots support (the Tea Party, etc.) for the oligarchy's agenda – the same dismantling of the government that GOP conservatives favor. He and his allies have spent more than three decades building out a framework for implementing their vision of American society and governance, "to undermine the normal governance of our democracy," per historian Nancy MacLean. "One such manifesto calls for a 'hostile takeover' of Washington, DC."

Elon Musk, however, has now ascended above Koch.

It's not hard to recognize that these three groups have much in common: they all represent people who fall short of a majority, but who believe that they, not the majority, should call the shots for society. They all demonize not only democracy, which stands opposed to their respective agendas, but government itself, which they believe should not be in the business of protecting and assisting the American public. And they all seek to entrench their power permanently, once they take it, by obliterating those laws, rules, and agencies that are in a position to stop or overthrow them.

It's also not hard to recognize that there is great overlap between them: many if not most GOP conservatives identify as Evangelical Christians; and Evangelical Christians are fine with demonizing anyone the GOP considers a threat to their power. The oligarchy has recruited Evangelical leaders into service – Jerry Falwell, Ralph Reed and others, oligarchs themselves, with their own business empires – to gin up public support.

With all this muscle, money and determination, it's astonishing that they haven't already succeeded. But it's important to note that despite their common ground, these three groups don't overlap to the degree that they seem to.

A major component of conservative ideology and Christian nationalism is shared aversion to Others – immigrants, foreigners in general, and persons of other religions. This aversion is a key trigger in stirring up fear that drives their constituencies to the polls. But the oligarchy couldn't care less; they have no interest at all in nationalism, and indeed see it as an obstruction: they are pursuing the very globalism that conservatives and Evangelicals abhor – one vast global market, with free exchange in all directions, where they can engage in border-free exploitation. This key ideological difference, alongside their very limited numbers, has been a barrier to the lockstep coordination their plans require.

Ultimately, that's just a detail. If democracy falls, all bets are off.

They long to end democracy – and are determined to get it done, and soon.

Oligarchy:
Plutocrats on the March

As with Christian Nationalists and the GOP, we can gauge the seriousness of the Oligarchy's threat to take over the federal government of the United States by the openness with which they declare their intent.

But it's important to note that the Oligarchy's threat differs from the other two. The GOP and the Christian Nationalists *intend* to take control of the federal government; the Oligarchy has *already done so.*

"The US is dominated by a rich and powerful elite," according to a study by Martin Gilens of Princeton University and Benjamin Page of Northwestern University. "Multivariate analysis indicates that economic elites and organised groups representing business interests have substantial independent impacts on US government policy, while average citizens and mass-based interest groups have little or no independent influence."

Their specific findings:

"A proposed policy change with low support among economically elite Americans (one-out-of-five in favour) is adopted only about 18% of the time," they write, "while a proposed change with high support (four-out-of-five in favour) is adopted about 45% of the time."

On the other hand, "When a majority of citizens disagrees with economic elites and/or with organised interests, they generally lose. Moreover, because of the strong status quo bias built into the US political system, even when fairly large majorities of Americans favour policy change, they generally do not get it."

"American democracy is a sham, no matter how much it's pumped by the oligarchs who run the country (and who control the nation's 'news' media)," wrote Eric Zuess in *Counterpunch*, commenting on the study for the BBC. "The US, in other words, is basically similar to Russia or most other dubious 'electoral' 'democratic' countries. We weren't formerly, but we clearly are now."

'Perhaps we ought to suck it up, admit we have a classist society and do like England where we have a House of Lords and a House of Commoners,' wrote Robyn Pennacchia for *Death and Taxes*, also quoted by the BBC. "Instead of pretending as though we all have some kind of equal opportunity here."

Jeffrey Winters, Professor of Political Science at Northwestern, put it this way:

"We're in a moment in the United States where that floodgate has been completely thrown open," he said. "There are now almost no limitations on the use of wealth in American democracy, and that means that what we have in the United States is a combination of democracy and oligarchy."

Gilens and Page make additional observations in their report:

"It is well established that organized groups regularly lobby and fraternize with public officials; move through revolving doors between public and private employment; provide self-serving information to officials; draft legislation; and spend a great deal of money on election campaigns."

"The oligarchs who largely took over America's political system in the 1980s drew mostly from the Charles and David Koch strain of libertarians," wrote Thom Hartmann in *The Hidden History of American Oligarchy*. "David had run for vice president on the Libertarian ticket in 1980 on a platform of privatizing Social Security, ending Medicare and Medicaid, ending the Environmental Protection Agency (EPA) and all antipollution efforts, privatizing the US Postal Service and pretty much every other government-provided service, and ending free public schools, all while cutting taxes on billionaires to nearly zero.

"As numerous writers have documented, the Koch brothers raised up a network that spanned the country, helping elect politicians in every state house and senate in the country, as well as cementing control over the Republican Party and the US Senate, most recently via their Tea Party," he continued. "The result has been that, since 1981, the GOP has opposed virtually every form of government function, government preparation, and government taxation to pay for both."

The question before us, then, is not one of taking control of government; it's the follow-up: will the

Oligarchy end democracy?

The Oligarch's Playbook

One way to approach the question of Oligarchy's intent is to examine its playbook, comparing it to that of other oligarchs who have seized control of governments elsewhere in the world.

"The transition from democracy to oligarchy usually starts with the very wealthy acquiring political power by buying influence with elected officials," wrote Hartmann. "They typically justify this with a belief that oligarchy is more stable and less messy than democracy, and that their success demonstrates that a sort of Darwinian process has chosen them to lead.

"From there, they begin to so completely control the mechanisms of information (the media) and campaigns (financing campaigns directly, as well as indirectly via third-party groups) that their agenda overwhelms the governing agenda.

"In the final stages, oligarchs themselves—or people so tightly aligned with them that they could only be called agents of particular oligarchs—rise up through seemingly democratic processes and take complete or near-complete control of government.

"From there, oligarchs typically begin to, as Steve Bannon said was the main goal of the Trump administration, 'deconstruct the administrative state,' seizing control over and corrupting every subordinate agency of government, from those responsible for enforcing the laws and the courts, to regulatory agencies, to those controlling the nation's currency and economy.

That playbook again:

- **Buying influence.** The Supreme Court's *Citizens United* ruling, check;
- **Control the media.** Fox News, the Murdoch media empire et al, check;
- **Seize the courts.** Trump SCOTUS appointments Neil Gorsuch, Brett Kavanaugh, and Amy Coney Barrett, check;
- **Annex a major political party.** The GOP, circa 1980s, check;
- **Take control of government itself.** Project 2025, pending.

The plutocrats are on the march. They have assumed control of the United States, and democracy itself is on the line.

Before Oligarchy:
Natural Humans

Looking around at all the tyrants thriving in the world today, and having now experienced one in our own White House, it's easy to assume that this is just the way it goes, and we've been lucky to have gone so long without one.

But it's not a trivial concern: many Americans, particularly in leadership, have long assumed, passively, that it can't happen here – and now we know that's not true. Far worse, we now know that an uncomfortable portion of our citizenry is just fine with an authoritarian in power. We must now be more vigilant than we've ever been.

It's also a mistake to assume it has always been so. But that turns out not to be the case; for most of the time modern humans have existed, social dominance has not been an issue.

In the near-term of our existence – the millennia since civilization was established – social dominators in various dress have emerged in pursuit of wealth and power. They take what they please, and manipulate the society in which they rise to empower themselves to preserve what they've taken. Put another way, they want it all, and they are willing to do whatever they must to have it.

But for the previous 250,000 years, that didn't happen. The emergence of tyrants wasn't a thing.

The archaeologist Bruce Trigger noted that "general acquisitiveness", as a component of human nature, is much more easily controlled in small societies than large ones. Those who surrender to a strong acquisitive drive are called *aggrandizers* by archaeologist Brian Hayden, who defines them as "any ambitious enterprising, aggressive, accumulative individual who strives to become dominant in a community, especially by economic means."

Small societies that mimic the communities of the Paleolithic era – living hunter-gatherer tribes – demonstrate this principle, per the research of David Erdal and Andrew Whiten, cited (as are Trigger and Hayden) by Jim O'Reilly in *Capitalism as Oligarchy*.

"It is characteristic of hunter-gatherers that they bring back to earth, often with a bump, anyone who tries to achieve dominance," they wrote. "The early human mind is likely to have been characterized by psychological dispositions supporting egalitarianism: vigilant food-sharing, informal leadership and counter-dominant behavior." Dominance by an alpha was strategically suppressed, according to anthropologist Christophe Boehm.

Put another way, if very small communities had remained the norm for human societies, tyranny would be unknown. If civilization had bequeathed us an endless procession of tiny towns, with no potential for obscene inequality and mis-distributed authority, none of our current mess – and none of what has tainted our existence for the past several thousand years – would have happened. There could be no Donald Trump in Mayberry.

"Small societies seem to have kept the alpha at bay," wrote O'Reilly, "but as they grew and became capable of producing and storing significant levels of surplus production, the previously successful defense mechanisms were undermined. The dominant long-lived egalitarian social organization of humanity shifted to one of unequal, hierarchical, class-based stratification. We don't know how it all transpired but given the brutal hierarchies that were to come, it's clear we're dealing with a catastrophic loss of human freedom."

The crushing irony is that most people are Andy and Barney and Aunt Bee and Opie and Thelma Lou and Floyd the Barber and Goober and Ernest T. Bass – people happy to live in harmony, with no interest in power over others or great wealth. Despite the constant flood of news that reinforces our awareness of the inequality all around us, most people are fine with live-and-let-live and just having what they need to care for their families and enjoy their lives. It's the handful who must have more, and will endlessly exploit others to get it – the Trumps, the authoritarians – that are at the root of it all.

The Nature of Oligarchy

Portrait of an Aligarchy

The word *oligarchy* pops up more frequently these days than it used to in political commentary – referring, of course, to rule of a society by a small, powerful minority group with access to great wealth, consequently exerting great influence. We hear that word a lot these days because wealth in the US – the world's richest country – has been wildly redistributed upward over the past four decades, empowering the richest 10% of the richest 1% beyond belief. This is alarming in itself, but it raises the question of just how powerful these uber-wealthy have become, as a result of their unimaginable resources.

Are we in the United States really, in fact, being quietly ruled by the wealthiest among us? Is that just hyperbole, or do they really have the power and influence to shape US law and the economy to their own liking, whether we like it or not?

If so, it's by no means a new thing. The wealthiest among us have always held disproportionate sway over countless societies since the concept of property first emerged more than 10,000 years ago, when agriculture was invented. Oligarchy may be the oldest form of government in the history of civilization.

There is strong evidence that the US is, in fact, a functional oligarchy, and that the oligarchy has intensified and grown vastly more powerful in just the past few years.

The rapid increase in the wealth of the wealthiest is a product of the COVID-19 Pandemic, which ravaged the world from 2019 to 2022, and which is still not fully abated. Before the pandemic hit, the wealth of US billionaires Jeff Bezos, Bill Gates, and Warren Buffett equaled the total wealth of the bottom half of all US citizens. According to the Institute for Policy Studies, the combined wealth of America's 725 billionaires increased from $2.9 trillion to $5 trillion in just the 18 months between March 2020 and October 2021. The top 10% of the top 1% possess 90% of all the wealth in the US.

So, yes, we've got some serious oligarchs in the US. And they have financial power beyond belief. But are they the ones pulling our strings?

Since the Roberts Court handed down its *Citizens United* decision in 2010, barriers to the financial influence of the elite class in US elections have all but collapsed. Billionaires contributed $2.6 billion to election campaigns in 2020, up from a comparatively paltry $31 million in 2010.

The billionaires in control of just three US companies – BlackRock, Vanguard and State Street – control more than $20 trillion in assets, a number matching the entire GDP of the nation. Those same major stockholders possess interest in 96% of the S&P 500; BlackRock, Vanguard and State Street are the largest shareholders in JPMorgan Chase, Citibank, and Wells Fargo, as well as Delta, United, American, and Southwest. They own 20 percent of Big Pharma. They are the largest stockholders in US media – Comcast, Warner Bros., and Disney.

Per Thom Hartmann, oligarchs have tried to install themselves in formal control of the country twice before – replacing democratic rule with their own autocratic governance – during the 1860s and again in the 1920s. Hartmann points to the past two decades, and the Trump Administration in particular, to emphasize that a third attempt is underway.

That's the driving force, he argues, behind Fox News; behind the tireless efforts of neoliberals to deregulate business; behind breathtakingly irresponsible tax cuts; behind the assault on any and all forms of public assistance; behind MAGA; behind the Roberts Court.

He identifies three key steps oligarchs must take to overthrow the democratic state and install their own autocracy:

- Control the media;
- Relax the consequences of bribery, to assert control over legislators;
- Control the court system, to alter or overturn legal process.

Several key developments in US law have been part of these three steps. Reagan rescinded the Fairness Doctrine in 1987, which had given political candidates equal time to present themselves on US airwaves for almost 40 years. The Telecommunications Act of 1996, signed by a president anxious to get next to business to counter the Gingrich Congressional revolution, removed protections set up for local television stations, radio stations and newspapers to prevent their acquisition by powerful corporations. And *Citizens United* removed barriers put in place many decades ago to obstruct special interests from seizing influence over lawmakers and legislative processes.

"Last week, the Supreme Court reversed a century of law to open the floodgates for special interests – including foreign corporations – to spend without limits in our elections," President Obama reported in the subsequent State of the Union address. In the years since, that's exactly what's happened.

What can be done about the growing power of the US oligarchy? Stemming the tide of MAGA and its authoritarian gestalt is a positive step, as is prosecuting to the fullest extent of the law the participants in the Jan. 6 assault on the US Capitol. Pushing back against this kind of faux revolution, which stirs just the sort of chaos that oligarchs eyeing the burial of democracy can exploit, is essential.

President Joe Biden aggressively worked to restore the Middle Class, which was a bulwark against oligarchy – an educated class with sufficient leisure to absorb and study current events and achieve an understanding of the workings of our economic and legal systems, and the insight to interpret them. That was a positive step, but an insufficient one; the US electorate chose Donald Trump, himself an oligarch, to succeed Biden.

We have, for the moment, career public servants in the justice system who are putting their careers on the line to push back against authoritarian abuses of high office – election fraud in particular – which can only strengthen that system, reinforcing the rule of law as a barrier against oligarchy encroachment.

Will it be enough? We can't know for sure; but if nothing else, it's all far more transparent than it was 20 years ago, 40 years ago. The important thing is to keep paying close attention, and remain aware of what's happening and how dangerous it can become.

The Threat of the Oligarch

Why is it important to understand oligarchy, its nature, and its potential impact? Why not give the oligarchs their due, and allow them their privilege?

Many, in fact, are happy to leave it at that. In any modern nation, there will be a significant proportion of average citizens who see the ultra-rich as deserving of their riches, and grant them their power on the assumption that their wealth is indicative of some nebulous competence that justifies their dominance.

But history has repeatedly shown that oligarchies are a great danger to any society in which they take root.

Here are some of oligarchy's perils, born out in even a superficial study of world history:

- **Concentration of power.** Political and economic power over all is held by a small group of elites who are unaccountable to those over whom they hold that power.
- **Lack of transparency.** Oligarchs carry out their activities beyond view of those who might object and take action against them, if those activities were publicly exposed.
- **Disparities of wealth.** The oligarch's goal is to become richer and to acquire more power and influence, in defense of that wealth; it is to the oligarch's advantage to maintain economic inequalities that disempower potential opponents in the lower classes.

- **Corruption.** Oligarchs tend to be corrupt, willing to wield influence in their acquisitive pursuits by buying the cooperation of policymakers and political influencers; they are likewise inclined to install their own loyalists in those positions for self-protection.
- **Self-Interest.** Oligarchs will use their power and influence to craft law and policy that favors their interests, with little or no concern for the impact on the population as a whole.
- **Limited social mobility.** Oligarchs exercise their social power and influence in such a way as to truncate the social mobility of the other classes – again, as a wealth defense measure.
- **Economic and social instability.** As oligarchs acquire more and more power and influence, securing their positions by actively widening social and economic inequalities, they foster instabilities in a society's systems that erode trust in institutions and promote class divisions, resulting in civil unrest.
- **Erosion of law.** What laws they can't change, oligarchs will evade, finding ways to shield themselves – and thereby weakening the rule of law overall. This can include the manipulation of the judicial system, in which they embed their own loyalists or jurists amenable to their influence – undermining justice overall.

- **Environmental destruction.** Those made fabulously wealthy by industrial means have demonstrated for many decades that short-term profit is of far greater importance to them than environmental stability. This is dangerous not only to the communities in which they operate, but the world overall.

This is quite a list, of course, and when taken as a whole demonstrate that unchecked, unlimited wealth in the hands of unconstrained people is a great danger to the societies they inhabit. It's a wonder, given the lengthy and detailed history of oligarchs across the centuries, that their presence is still tolerated, let alone accommodated.

Oligarchy's Deep History

Rule of, by, and for the rich has been part of the human story for millennia. The word *oligarchy* itself was coined by Aristotle, establishing Ancient Greece as its starting point. It served to distinguish a ruling class beyond mere aristocracy, which largely referred to rule by the qualified – a ruling class defined by wealth and power that was not necessarily considerate of the good of the people.

Oligarchy spread to the Roman Republic, where wealthy patricians exercised disproportionate influence over public affairs, rolling forward into Europe's evolving feudal systems, where control of lands represented a wealth that came with political voice. There was born the oligarchic cleric, made wealthy de facto by the church, able to control the politics of nations where the church held sway.

It took a major leap forward in the city-states of Italy, where modern finance was born, and control of trade and capital fell into the hands of the most affluent. It also advanced family-based oligarchy, wherein powerful families like the de Medicis exercised overwhelming influence, not just at home, but in neighboring nations.

The United Kingdom advanced oligarchy still further with the invention of the corporation, a state-chartered arm of empire; British Corporations like the East India Company were created to advance British interests by opening up trade routes and developing new markets, which the British nobility freely exploited. The actions of the East India Company itself could have greater impact on the economy and policies of a trading partner nation than its British ambassador.

And it was by way of such British corporations that oligarchy made itself known in the American colonies – where British agency for British wealth drew resentment from the colonists. In a land where it was not yet possible to amass great wealth or capital, there was no capacity for any concentration of power that could push back. Nor, in the fledgling American society, were there any social hierarchies supporting rungs high enough to compete with British economic and political power.

Oligarchy and the Framers

America's Constitutional Framers – Ben Franklin, John Adams, Thomas Jefferson, James Madison et al – knew oligarchy when they saw it.

It manifested in their embryonic coastal cities, where ports administrated by their mother country received goods and materials from Britain and other European trading partners. It manifested in the taxes imposed on those goods and materials by the British crown and the British corporations that served as the crown's agents. And they were certainly well-acquainted with the oligarchies that flourished in France and other European monarchies.

Being highly educated, well-traveled, and socially well-connected men, the Framers had strong opinions about the oligarchies they observed – and with the concept of oligarchy itself.

"At the outset of the American republic, when the Framers of the United States Constitution first submitted the document to the public for approval, the question of oligarchy was hotly debated," wrote Luke Mayville in *John Adams and the Fear of American Oligarchy*. "Crisis of the Constitution – the so-called Anti-Federalists – argued that the new system would elevate to power a wealthy ruling class. Rather than empowering those 'who had been used to walk in the plain and frugal paths of life,' the new system of government would guarantee rule by America's 'Aristocracy.' What the Constitution's defenders had fancifully called 'representative democracy' would in fact be 'a mere burlesque.' There would be 'no part of the people represented, but the rich,' and no security provided against the undue influence of a social and economic elite.

"Meanwhile, Federalist proponents of the Constitution argues that there was little reason to view the rich as a dangerous political force," Mayville continued. "After all, the aristocratic orders of the Old World were absent in post-Revolution America, and the Constitution mandated that this remain the case by expressly prohibiting title of nobility. America would be a *republic*, and the real danger in republics was not oligarchic power but the power of untrammeled majorities. James Madison, whose influence at the Philadelphia Convention was second to none, warned against 'the superior force of an interested and over-bearing majority.' In his monumental 10th essay in the *Federalist Papers*, Madison paid only passing attention to the danger that an oligarchic elite could pose. Being small in numbers, such an elite would simply be voted down. Oligarchic power might exist as a nuisance, but it would not be a serious threat to the republic: 'It may clog the administration, it may convulse the society; but it will be unable to execute and mask its violence under the forms of the Constitution.' In a revolutionary republic that had thrown off aristocracy and monarchy and put 'We the People' on the throne, there was no reason to feat oligarchy.

"When Federalists and Anti-Federalists debated the likelihood of oligarchy in America, they were partaking in a larger, transatlantic discourse about how best to ameliorate the vast inequality of political power that had characterized the aristocratic societies of 18th-century Europe. The emerging democratic-republican consensus, espoused by an increasingly influential set of reformers in France and several other European nations, held that the key to eliminating aristocratic privilege was the dismantling of the various forms of *legal* privilege found in European societies. Orders of nobility, titles, social ranks or 'estates,' hereditary magistracies – these were the pillars that propped up aristocratic privilege. Pulling down such pillars would be the essential step in breaking aristocratic power and establishing true republics, formed upon the basis of equal citizenship.

"From the perspective of the American Federalists, the Constitution of 1787 would establish just the type of republic envisioned by European reformers. The proposed American system prohibited titles of nobility and – remarkably in the context of the 18th century – made no distinction between the rich and the poor. In this context, what did Anti-Federalists mean when they spoke of a home-grown aristocracy? They agreed that America would be home to an aristocracy in the ancient-Greek sense of *hoi aristoi* (the best), a class of men distinguished by meritocratic qualities such as talent and virtue. But with the entrenched aristocratic orders of the Old World completely absent in America, the fear of a dangerous aristocracy or oligarchy of corrupt elites was without foundation.

"Yet leading Federalist and European reformers alike tended to overlook a dissenting view of elite power. In the American context, many Anti-Federalists believed that the roots of political inequality ran deeper than was assumed and that aristocratic power would survive the dismantling of formal aristocratic institutions. When Anti-Federalists used the term 'aristocracy,' they meant something quite different from the conventional aristocracy of the Old World. Though formal aristocratic orders would no exist in the new republic, American would remain threatened by an oligarchic elite consisting of 'birth, education, talents, and wealth,' a class that would tend to monopolize political power. This class, which Anti-Federalists insisted on calling an aristocracy, would lac the trappings of European nobility but would nonetheless enjoy distinctions 'as visible and of as much influence as titles, stars, and garters.'"

This was a new idea – an oligarchy arising not from an established order, but from the grass roots. An oligarchy composed of men who simply decided to pursue wealth at all costs, and were willing to work within a system that gave them no formal recognition but from which they could extract the same rewards as their European counterparts – fortune, power and influence, and societal dominance.

It was hotly debated, but there was no Framer who didn't have firm opinions on the issue. Here are some of those opinions.

Thomas Jefferson

Jefferson called this new kind of oligarchy a *natural aristocracy*, and shared his thoughts about it with both John Adams and James Madison. In an 1813 letter to Adams, he wrote:

"The natural progress of things is for liberty to yield and government to gain ground. The tendency of power to corrupt, and the propensity of the few to seek to control the many, has been, in every age, a constant, unyielding truth."

Put another way, Jefferson saw the propensity for some men to pursue wealth and power for the sake of social dominance as built into the human species – and therefore a danger to the republic they were committed to creating.

He called out oligarchy specifically in a 1798 letter to John Taylor, declaring it a form of tyranny:

""I have sworn upon the altar of God eternal hostility against every form of tyranny over the mind of man. And I will continue to oppose every form of tyranny over the mind of man, and every form of tyranny over the body of man, including the tyranny of oligarchy."

Moreover, he viewed the distribution of lands in the New World – the ownership of property by common people – as a hedge against a takeover by wealthy elites. If the federal government promoted and supported an agrarian nation with a healthy class of independent farmers, the dangers of concentrated power in the hands of elites were less likely to present. He articulated this in a 1789 letter to James Madison:

"The acquisition of the country's lands, and the enjoyment of them by a people who are independent and virtuous, will keep the government in its proper form, and maintain the liberties of the country."

John Adams

"Shall we conclude, from these melancholy observations, that human nature is incapable of liberty, that no honest equality can be preserved in society, and that such forcible causes are always at work as must reduce all men to a submission to despotism, monarchy, oligarchy, or aristocracy? By no means!" ~John Adams, in his 1787 *Defense of the Constitutions of Government of the United States*.

And this:

"When economic power became concentrated in a few hands, then political power flowed to those possessors and away from the citizens, ultimately resulting in an oligarchy or tyranny." ~from *On the Importance of Property Distribution*, 1776.

James Madison

One of Madison's justifications for a large republic, offered in *Federalist No. 10*, was its capacity to contain emerging oligarchies better than a small republic. A large republic with a diverse population would simply be much more difficult for a small group of elites to dominate:

"Extend the sphere, and you take in a greater variety of parties and interests; you make it less probable that a majority of the whole will have a common motive to invade the rights of other citizens."

In *Federalist No. 51*, he came alongside Jefferson in considering concentrated power among the view a definition of tyranny:

"In every government, there are points in which the liberties of the people are exposed to danger. The concentration of power in the hands of a few, however well intentioned, has always led to corruption and tyranny."

In a letter to Jefferson, he wrote that wealthy elites tend to influence public policy in their own favor, distorting the principle of democracy:

"The object of government is to protect the minority of the opulent against the majority."

The Framers understood oligarchy and its dangers very well, having observed it up close throughout their lives as colonial citizens. And it was against that oligarchy that they rose up in the 1770s, declaring their independence and going to war to secure it.

But they didn't vanquish oligarchy by any means. It could not have been clear at the time, but they were setting in motion a cycle that would persist in their new democracy from that day forward – a cycle in which oligarchs would themselves rise up and patient work toward a day when they could take that democracy away.

The Indigenous Critique

More than a few voices in paleontology and anthropology have suggested that Paleolithic humans were not at all savage and did not practice social dominance, but were instead egalitarian in their social order and equality-minded in their economics – owing, more than anything, to their lack of the concept of "property" or "wealth". What happened to one, happened to all; the members of any given human tribe were all in it together.

Civilization, originating in the Fertile Crescent and spreading throughout the Middle East in all directions, put an end to that. Agriculture, for all its power to feed more people and make possible the long-term storage of food – surplus – also bestowed the concepts of property and wealth, ownership, and stratified society. It was a very mixed blessing.

And when civilized humans began crossing the oceans and made their way to the Americas, they were closing that circle: humans who had lived through 200 generations of civilization, with its kings and armies and religions and treasures and poverty and slavery and genocides, found themselves face-to-face with humans who were *still in their Edenic state* – latter-day Paleoliths, still living according to Nature's laws, unsullied by wealth and property and class and autocracy.

Those humans included the Wendat, better known to history as the Huron tribe of the Iroquois Confederacy, encountered by French Jesuit missionaries who had hiked into Canada to save their souls. They were astonished by what they found.

"I do not believe there is any people on earth freer than they, and less able to allow the subjection of their wills to any power whatever," wrote Father Lallemant in *Jesuit Relations* in 1644, "so much so that Fathers here have no control over their children, or Captains over their subjects, or the Laws of the Country over any of them, except in so far as each is pleased to submit to them. There is no punishment which is inflicted on the guilty, and no criminal who is not sure that his life and property are in no danger."

How did the Wendat achieve this? "Consent of the governed" – the principle that would makes its way to Thomas Jefferson by way of Locke and Rousseau.

Governance among the Wendat was achieved through simple dialog and debate – smart people disagreeing.

"When the governed agreed, decisions were made or punishments meted out," Hartmann writes. "When they didn't, things were worked out in dialogue and debate, sometimes lasting days."

"This form of justice restrains all of these peoples, and seems more effectually to repress disorders than the personal punishment of criminals does in France," Lallemant wrote.

These writings took Europe by storm, triggering an insatiable curiosity about Native Americans that persisted for decades.

"I can say in truth that, as regards intelligence, they are in no wise inferior to Europeans and to those who dwell in France. I would never have believed that, without instruction, nature could have supplied a most ready and vigorous eloquence, which I have admired in many Hurons; or more clear-sightedness in public affairs, or a more discreet management in things to which they are accustomed."

The Baron De Lahontan, a Dutchman, would write, half a century later, of his dialogs with "an unusually brilliant Wendat statesman named Kandiaronk." His writings took up where the Jesuits had left off, giving Europe another look into the lives of humans still in Nature's arms, untouched by the afflictions of civilization. Ben Franklin was busy being born as those writings spread across Europe like wildfire, going through a dozen reprintings in a wide array of languages – and setting in motion the pens of the Enlightenment philosophers in Britain and France.

De Lahontan's dialog with his Wendat companion surfaced many criticisms of European society, overall a scathing indictment. Lahontan described Native America's own social order with astonishment:

"They think it unaccountable that one man should have more than another, and that the rich should have more respect than the poor. In short, they say, the name of 'savages', which we bestow upon them, would fit ourselves better, since there is nothing in our actions that bears an appearance of wisdom."

A 19-year-old Thomas Jefferson would meet such a Native American leader face to face – the Cherokee diplomat Ontasseté, who spent a great deal of time in colonial cities and towns, and would travel to England to negotiate a treaty with King George II. He and his brother Framers were very clear on the concepts by which these out-of-time people lived, how they managed their society. And it was on those ideas that they built the first true democracy in the civilized world.

We face the rise of the Authoritarian in the West today because we haven't gone far enough in the direction of either the Native America of the past or the Bartlet vision of the future. One of our commitments must be, not only to the principle of governance by the consent of the governed, but the uncompromising practice of universal social and economic equality among the governed.

Oligarchy in the US: A Long Cycle

Oligarchies do not arise overnight; they form over generations, quietly amassing influence and position and resources. By the time they are in place, in control of a society, it is often too late to do anything about them; they possess all the machinery of power, and have the means to maintain it.

That has been the story in the United States since the nation's founding. As mentioned above, the revolution fought by the Founders was to rid the colonies of a despotic monarch, George III, and to get out from under the economic power of an oligarchy – represented by the British East India Company.

And so began what historian Thom Hartmann has defined as a cycle – a perpetual effort of the wealthy, within the United States, to establish an oligarchy and take overt control of the government and the economy.

The cycle, as Hartmann observes in The *Hidden History of American Oligarchy*, begins with the US citizenry asserting itself in opposition to oligarchy and proceeding to propagate an economy and governance that are as favorable to ordinary citizens as possible.

"Typically, major shocks bring about rapid and major change," he wrote. "The financial panic of 1770 helped precipitate the American Revolution; the great crash of 1856 brought the Southern oligarchy to a head, leading to the Civil War and the abolition of slavery; the Republican Great Depression of 1930 led straight to the New Deal and major anti-oligarchic reforms."

These periods of prosperity, Hartmann notes, last more than a generation, less than two.

At around the 40-year mark, a new oligarchy will have formed, exploiting the rules in place at the time, and will begin the slow work of tipping both the economy and government in its own direction. This effort, too, will last between one and two generations – about another 40 years.

At the 80-year mark, that oligarchy tries to assert dominance, triggering a national confrontation. Democracy and oligarchy face off, with the future of the nation at stake.

This cycle, Hartmann documents, has occurred three times in the nation's history: the period between the Revolutionary War and the Civil War; the period from the Civil War to the New Deal; and the period from the New Deal to today (2024, at this writing).

The intermittent 40-year markers were the 1820s, when oligarchs seized control of industry in the South; the peak of the Gilded Age, when oligarchs again scrambled for control (and largely got it), leading to the Crash of '29; and the Reagan Revolution, when after 40 years of middle class prosperity, a new oligarchy spurred a government embrace of neoliberal policies, hollowing out that middle class and greatly empowering that new oligarchy – the wealthiest and most powerful in history.

And today, we have reached the 80-year mark in Hartmann's cycle – 80 years since the end of World War II and the flourishing of New Deal prosperity; 40 years since this new oligarchy began to make its move.

It's confrontation time...

Oligarchy and the Civil War

With the creation of the United States of America, the Framers of its Constitution had instituted a new era – a new age in which all men were created equal – ostensibly, anyway – and the thousands of years of rich ones ruling over poor ones was ended. The new nation made a modest beginning in this unique enterprise, but the principle had been firmly embraced.

The on-paper equality of citizens was more easily declared than industrial equality was achieved along the Atlantic coastline, as the resource-rich northern states enjoyed rapid and prosperous development while the agrarian South, less resource-laden, struggled to tame its lands. It was, in other words, harder to get rich in the South than in the North.

As has happened so often in the history of oligarchy, new technology rapidly altered the economic landscape. In 1794, Eli Whitney invented a machine into which raw cotton could be dumped, and with the turning of a drum, the seeds in the cotton could be screened out. The 'cotton gin' revolutionized that industry, according to Hartmann: "Now that one machine could clean as much cotton as fifty people, every cotton plantation faced the possibility that it could produce 50 times as much cotton (and profit), if only it had 50 times as much land to grow the cotton on and 50 times as many people to pick it."

This threw open the floodgates for the Southerners who were wealthiest at the time; by buying up that land, and buying slaves to work it, they would become

50 times as wealthy. That, of course, is the nature of the oligarch.

The impact of this new reality on slavery in the South, already in place for decades, and the state of democracy in that quarter of the new nation, can scarcely be overstated.

Hartmann quoted Illinois Representative John Farnsworth in an 1864 floor speech:

"[With t]he invention of the cotton-gin, the cultivation of cotton made it profitable to raise men and women for the southern market. The price of slaves was enhanced; from being worth $250 they went up to $1,200 and $1,300.

"Then the greed for power took possession of the slave-holders, and the avarice of these men overleaped itself and they became clamorous for the extension of slavery. The bounds were too narrow for them. They became ambitious of a nation that should be founded upon 'the cornerstone of slavery.'

"Then it was, Mr. Speaker, that the slave power got the control of the Government, of the executive, legislative, and judicial departments. Then it was that they got possession of the high places of society. They took possession of the churches. They took possession of the lands. Then it became criminal for a man to open his lips in denunciation of the evil and sin of slaveholding.

"Then followed... the attempt to expel John Quincy Adams; the throttling of the right to petition; suppressing the freedom of the press; the suppression of the freedom of the mails; all these things followed the taking possession of the Government and lands by the slave power, until we were the slaves of slaves, being chained to the car of this slave Juggernaut...

"Then came the conventions of the rival political parties, in which they declared that the agitation of this vexed question should cease. But it would not cease, for the slave power was still clamoring for more, more, more!

"Then came the [Dred Scott] decision of the Supreme Court. Why, sir, the spirit of slavery took possession of that court and instigated the palsied arm of a judge upon the brink of the grave to attempt to snatch the charter of human liberty from the throne of the Almighty. The Southern oligarchs were on the rise."

By the 1830s, wrote Hartmann, "the South was firmly in the economic, political, and social hands of a small number of uber-wealthy plantation-based oligarchs made fabulously rich by the invention of the cotton gin."

He then quoted Forrest A. Nabors in his book *From Oligarchy to Republicanism: The Great Task of Reconstruction*:

"A new generation of rulers reshaped the South around their new ruling principle... The development of Southern oligarchy portended the rupture of the union, regardless of the ties that bound them together, because no ties, physical, legal, or otherwise, can overcome the difference between fundamentally opposed types of political regimes."

And he then quoted Senator Timothy Howe of Wisconsin, from an 1864 speech on the floor of the US House of Representatives:

"If the cotton gin had not been invented, slaveholding would not have been profitable. If slaveholding had not been profitable, slaveholders would not have been rich. If slaveholders had not been rich, they would not have been arrogant. If they had not been arrogant, 400,000 slaveholders would not have presumed to challenge dominion over 20 million freemen.

"Slavery without the cotton-gin would have been a monster wrong, but it would not have been dangerous to the Republic. The cotton gin without slavery would have been of twice the value it has been and still would not have been dangerous to anyone. Together they have proved fatal to the peace of the nation."

Farnsworth and Howe both took note that the commitment of the Southern oligarchs to the practice of slavery that enabled their obscene wealth pushed them to aspire to national rule – not merely to secure slavery in their own provinces, but to extend it throughout the North and West. And this, Hartmann wrote, brought about the Civil War.

"Such, then, I find to be the cause and the purpose of the rebellion," said Howe. "It was not to secure toleration for slavery within the seceding States, but to compel the adoption of slavery by the nation." In other words, the Confederacy rose up not simply to preserve Southern oligarchy, but to extend that oligarchy to the rest of the United States.

Civil war there was. President Abraham Lincoln, committed to the nation's survival and slavery's obsolescence, was unflinching in his leadership of a nation on the brink, even as 600,000 men died horribly. And the Southern oligarchy, of course, lost.

"The Civil War could thus be recast as a war between oligarchy and democracy, where democracy won by a whisker," Hartmann wrote.

Oligarchy: Gilded Age, Roaring Twenties

Thwarted by Lincoln and the Civil War, the Southern oligarchy made a bid, under Lincoln's successor Andrew Johnson, to reassert control over Washington DC – a bid that failed, obliging them to submit to a Reconstruction of the South instituted by Congress. An amended US Constitution freed the slaves, and the South was left to rebuild, according to rules set forth at the federal level.

The Compromise of 1877, brought about by a dispute over the presidential contest between Rutherford B. Hayes and Samuel Tilden, effectively ended Reconstruction. The Southern oligarchy persisted, albeit in a considerably weakened state.

As the broader industrial revolution swept the entire country through the remainder of the century, a new generation of oligarchs appeared in the final two decades of the 19th century. A Gilded Age emerged, in which the new wealth led to class divisions that rivaled those across the ocean in Europe.

An American aristocracy was emerging.

A Gilded Age

That aristocracy extended North to South, as industrialization and urban expansion, driven by proliferating railroads and dazzling new technologies like telephony and the electric light, showed exponential growth for years on end. Business boomed across the country, which was itself growing rapidly as the West opened up and new states were formed. That boom was a result of America's embrace of the private corporation.

British corporations had been a tool of state, opening doors for the expansion of its empire; they were deployed in the service of the British citizenry. The American version of the corporation had no such constraints; it was there for private use, a mechanism for enrichment of an individual (or a small group). Its relationship to the state was, ideally, mutual disinterest.

Per Edward O'Donnell, a history professor at College of the Holy Cross, more than 100,000 private corporations had been chartered in the US by 1870.

In what came to be known as the Gilded Age, America had become what the Framers had hoped it never would: a reflection of Europe's socioeconomic extremes, with its yawning wealth gap and growing poverty.

O'Donnell tells of a journalist named Henry George, who took an interest in the rising economic inequality in America and decided to write about it. His bestseller *Progress and Poverty* outlined the dilemma of rising poverty in the shadow of rising prosperity:

"Why, amid so many signs of economic progress, did poverty actually increase? Why wasn't everyone benefitting from the Industrial Revolution?

"George wrote, 'It is as though an immense wedge were being forced, not underneath society, but *through* society. Those who are above the point of separation are elevated, but those who are below are crushed down.'

"*Progress and Poverty* warned that the very fate of the republic was at stake. George wrote, 'This association of poverty with progress is the great enigma of our times. It is the riddle which the Sphynx of Fate puts to our civilization, in which not to answer is to be destroyed.'"

Americans trapped on the underside of the divide George articulated noted with increasing alarm that big business was making inroads into the democratic process, made clear in the scandals that erupted (like the Crédit Mobilier railroad incident of 1872 and the Whiskey Ring scandal of 1876) when they got caught. They also noted with growing dismay that Supreme Court rulings leaned increasingly toward big business and away from farmers and workers.

As the 20th century got underway, an era of robber barons had begun. Industrial titans such as John D. Rockefeller, Andrew Carnegie, Cornelius Vanderbilt, and JP Morgan dominated the oil, steel, railroad and finance industries respectively. Corporate trusts, which operate in favor of the oligarch and against an economy more suited to the average citizen, were flourishing, and there was little to constrain the proliferating monopolies that had emerged. Whoever was at the forefront of an industry enjoyed full control of that industry, and the federal government wasn't bothering to regulate them. It was an oligarch's heaven.

These industrialists controlled the political machinery of the nation, through lobbying, the purchase of politicians through campaign donations and outright bribery. Laws tended to favor business over citizens, prompting the rise of labor unions gearing up to fight back. Oligarchs controlled the major newspapers, triggering a surge in journalists and writers (like Upton Sinclair) seeking to expose corruption, exploitation, and social injustice.

This resistance coalesced into a progressive era that challenged the entrenched oligarchy, championed by President Teddy Roosevelt. The 13th Amendment passed, introducing the direct election of senators. Workers' rights were strengthened; antitrust legislation was passed (though insufficiently enforced). The regulation of industry became an increasingly prominent theme.

The progressive pushback, while well-intentioned, was for naught. As World War I shook up economies the world over, industrial innovation in the US threw open doors to new opportunity for its oligarchs, as the automobile, air travel, and the increasing electrification of the nation – all industries in themselves – stimulated growth in all the other industries. Trusts and monopolies continued unimpeded; worker welfare was of little concern to the titans controlling them.

By 1929, the top 1% of the nation possessed 40% of the nation's wealth.

Crash

A major source of that wealth was stock market speculation, one of many risky practices that the Presidents of the decade – Harding, Coolidge, and Hoover – were uninclined to regulate. In general, a laissez-faire attitude prevailed, which is exactly what the oligarchy wanted.

But it was much to their detriment, as this speculation drove a bubble that burst in October 1929, bringing down the market and triggering the collapse of the economy over the next four years.

Some oligarchs weathered the storm; some went broke. The system they had worked for decades to put in place for their own enrichment and security, however, was eradicated.

What's the Deal?

Elected on a promise to set things right in 1932, Franklin D. Roosevelt went right to work – presenting the nation with a New Deal. That New Deal regulated business, provided a social safety net, invested in public infrastructure, education for the common citizen, and worked to ensure the rights of all.

From Hartmann:[1] "Recognizing that a strong and robust middle class was the nation's best defense against oligarchy (in the speech, he referred to it as 'Fascism'), Roosevelt noted that 'these political rights proved inadequate to assure us equality in the pursuit of happiness.' That, he said, would require not just political rights for all Americans, but economic rights as well. 'We have come to a clear realization,' FDR said, 'of the fact that true individual freedom cannot exist without economic security and independence.'

---

[1] In *The Hidden History of American Oligarchy*.

Quoting himself from a 1936 campaign speech, he added, 'Necessitous men are not free men.'

"Rights are unusual and powerful things in those countries (like ours) where one of the main functions of government is to protect rights. As FDR pointed out, our political rights are largely protected, from free speech to the right to a trial by jury. But the right to have health care, a higher education, housing, or even a well-paying job? In America today, those are all privileges, not rights, so government has no obligation to either protect your access to them or supply them if the marketplace fails to.

"Shifting these things from being privileges to rights would be earth-shaking in the United States. Countries of the developed world took this step decades ago, most of them citing FDR's famous 1944 speech and making those changes after World War II, but every attempt to do so here in the United States has been successfully blocked by Republican conservative ideologues.

"However, FDR had the force of personality and political brilliance to pull it off, and the crisis of the Republican Great Depression and World War II to create an opening for its acceptance. So he began planting the first seeds with his constitutionally required annual State of the Union presentation.

"'In our day,' he said, 'these economic truths have become accepted as self-evident.' Americans, after all, loved their Social Security and unemployment benefits, and had learned from the contrast between Democratic and Republican policies that a strong social safety net was a key to the American Dream."

With the advent of the New Deal, oligarchy suffered its greatest defeat in history. So strong and far-reaching were its bulwarks that generations of effort have yet to overturn it (though efforts to do so are, even today, unceasing).

But on this second pass through the Hartmann cycle, more than 150 years into the American Experiment, the oligarchs had only themselves to blame: in the Civil War, Lincoln had defeated them on the battlefield; this time, they had actually won – and the oligarchy they created had collapsed from its own rot.

Oligarchy: The Reagan Revolution

In the wake of the economic cascade formed by the Crash of '29, the Great Depression, the New Deal, and World War II, the world's conservative philosophers and economics united with oligarchs in the US and Europe, via an event now referred to as the Walter Lippmann Colloquium, followed by the formation of the Mont Pelerin Society, to forge a new economic philosophy that could push back against the highly successful, highly egalitarian New Deal – a deal that was wonderful for average citizens, and not so much for oligarchs and corporations.

This marked the beginning of the cycle of oligarchy that is culminating today, in the 2020s.

The Walter Lippmann Colloquium

In August 1938, as World War II was poised to erupt in Europe, 26 intellectuals gathered in Paris at the behest of French philosopher Louis Rogier. Between them, they concocted a plan to fix the world. □

That there was much that needed fixing in the world in 1938 is obvious to the most casual reader of history, but the focus of Rogier's 26 was, in particular, to articulate defenses against rising socialism, collectivism, and *laissez-faire* liberalism. Given the world-wide ravages of the recent Great Depression, it was also felt that nationalism and isolationist policies in any Western nation were detrimental to the health of the overall world economy.

Joining Rogier in Paris was a veritable Who's Who of Western thinkers, including the Austrian-British philosopher Friedrich Hayek, Austro-Hungarian economist Ludwig von Mises, German sociologist Alexander Rüstow – and, most significantly, the US journalist/political commentator Walter Lippmann.

That they named their colloquium after Lippmann owed to his recent publication of his latest book, the widely-respected *An Enquiry into the Principles of the Good Society*, which was so admired that the assembled men took the time to study it there in Paris.[1] That book, which summarized the history of liberalism, had become a rallying cry against totalitarianism in the US. (Its predecessor *Public Opinion*, a study of how social perception and factors in media can weaken societal cohesion, was likewise lauded.)

Once they got down to it, these congregated minds found themselves divided into two distinct camps. The first, which included von Mises along with French economists Jacques Rueff and Étienne Mantoux and others, resisted the idea of jettisoning *laissez-faire* (completely free market) economics; the second, which included Hayek, Lippmann, Rüstow, French political scientist Raymond Aron and others, favored a system with a greater role for state intervention in societal development, and were not so set against government regulation.

They intended to call the product of their deliberations *neoliberalism* – 'new liberalism' - a term coined by Rüstow. Though they never achieved consensus on what it would represent there in Paris, the term persisted.

As interesting as this colloquium might be in political hindsight, it didn't come to much; though the group intended to continue, the war interrupted their efforts, and the major consequence of the Paris proceedings was that it inspired Hayek to form the Mont Pelerin Society almost a decade later.

Hayek essentially picked up where the earlier colloquium had left off. Established in Vevey, Switzerland in 1947, the Mont Pelerin Society – which included Hayek, Lippmann, von Mises, German economist Wilhelm Ropke and Hungarian philosopher of science Michael Polanyi from the earlier group – included US economist Milton Friedman and Austrian philosopher Karl Popper. The society was created to draft a charter for the emerging International Trade Organization, a body intended to create standards and practices in support of a viable global economy. That idea was very much in keeping, of course, with the original colloquium's mission of fostering a healthy universal economic climate that would stave off communism and lead to planetary prosperity.

In principle, both the Walter Lippmann Colloquium and the subsequent Mont Pelerin Society were laudable. They pursued the lofty goals of worldwide economic cooperation and improvement in the human condition at a time when such cooperation and improvement were sorely needed. The MPS expressed it this way:

Over large stretches of the Earth's surface the essential conditions of human dignity and freedom have already disappeared. In others they are under constant menace from the development of current tendencies of policy. The position of the individual and the voluntary group are progressively undermined by extensions of arbitrary power. Even that most precious possession of Western Man, freedom of thought and expression, is threatened by the spread of creeds which, claiming the privilege of tolerance when in the position of a minority, seek only to establish a position of power in which they can suppress and obliterate all views but their own.

~MPS Statement of Aims, April 1947

Neoliberalism now had a coherent definition.

The debate over *laissez-faire*, which had divided the members of the colloquium a decade earlier, carried over into the MPS. Should markets be left completely free of government regulation, or was some regulation necessary to enforce competitive order? Could corporations get too big, and wasn't regulation the best way to keep that from happening? Did government have any business engineering modern society, or should it be free to develop on its own? All of these questions were tackled with energy and spirited disagreement.

Neoliberalism has been the primary force shaping the world over the past four decades – and some historical context will hopefully enhance that discussion.

The Advent of Neoliberalism

The word "neoliberalism" is appearing with increasing frequency in the media, the writings of historian Heather Cox Richardson in particular (more from her below). We can credibly view it as the defining political agency of the 20th century, over communism, socialism, fascism and democracy, and it seems it is thrashing wildly beneath the current waves in Western society.

The term *neoliberalism* has no connection to our modern usage of the embedded word *liberal*, which we associate with *progressive democrat*. In this usage, *liberal* is closer to its root *liberty*, meaning *freedom*, more specifically *free of government*. It was coined by a group of laissez-faire economists in World War II Europe (Milton Friedman and Friedrich Hayek were among them; see above) and formalized by the Mont Pelerin Society.

This group sought to create economic blockades against communism in the West (a good thing) and foresaw the emerging globalization of markets (also a good thing). Their ideology called for extreme deregulation of national economies to facilitate that globalization, based on the assumption that unregulated markets would naturally coalesce.

Reaganism

The machinery of neoliberalism came into being through these events, and while the US middle class was flourishing and the economy was expanding and the national standard of living, education, and health soared to record highs, it was focused on undoing these impediments to the oligarchs' advance.

Per Thom Hartmann, the overwhelming failure of Barry Goldwater's bid for the presidency in the wake of John F. Kennedy's assassination was a wake-up call to the growing oligarchy that a new game plan was needed.

"America's third struggle with oligarchy," he wrote, "Began in 1971, when Lewis Powell, himself a proud agent of the tobacco oligarchs, laid out in a famous memo to the US Chamber of Commerce a plan for the various oligarchs of America to stop competing and organize to take over the US government. By 1980, the plan was in full flower."

That plan, which came to fruition with the election of Ronald Reagan, led to a neoliberal era in the US – an era that began in 1981 and is still in force today.

Next, "America's oligarchs succeeded in getting enough of their guys placed on the Supreme Court to legalize political bribery (in 1976 and 1978 in the Buckley and Bellotti decisions50) for the first time in American history. That event opened the door to this generation's oligarchic control of all three branches of government via the Reagan Revolution and the billionaire takeover of the GOP."

'Reaganism' isn't really a word, of course, but his occupancy of the White House was a defining moment for both neoliberalism and America's slide toward authoritarianism. He walked neoliberal ideology through the nation's front door, opening touting its tenets and aggressively leveraging them to dismantle the work of FDR and Eisenhower.

The new president started touting 'trickle-down' as a solution to the national economy's burps and bumps. It was the first shot in an assault that rapidly became relentless, as he and his allies not only took aim at federal policy, but at public perception of the government. The Reagan presidency was one of unceasing neoliberal messaging.

Those messages are easily summarized:

- The US government is your enemy;
- The government needs to get out of the business of helping Americans;
- The well-being of business transcends the national interest;
- *Deregulate, deregulate, deregulate!*

Ronald Reagan was a juggernaut on all these fronts, setting the tone and strategy for all in the GOP who would follow him.

His assaults on the democratic order weren't just systematic and persistent; they were overt, out in the open, often paraded on national television.

"Government is not the solution to our problem, government *is* the problem," he declared, followed later by, "The nine most terrifying words in the English language are: 'I'm from the government, and I'm here to help.'" – casually vilifying, at a stroke, the hundreds of thousands who *do* enter public service out of a deep desire and conviction to help others and contribute to the betterment of the nation.

Reagan's demonization of government, already a GOP staple, was perhaps the least of it; his valentine to capitalism, a gutting of tax policy that had been in place since World War II, requiring businesses and the very wealthy to contribute their fair share back to the economy that had enriched them, exploded the national debt. In cutting the top tax rate from 70% to 25%, he tripled it, from $738 billion to $2.4 trillion. That quickly, the US went from being the world's largest creditor to the world's largest debtor.

The justification was that the US economy wasn't functioning properly, but that wasn't true at all. The economy had boomed steadily during the post-World War II years, with only the normal fluctuations. The number of people in the US living in poverty had continually declined, even as the overall population rose.

In the process, Reagan and his allies laid track for the GOP to come by dissembling in the media to justify his agenda. His budget director, David Stockman, perpetuated the trickle-down gospel that cutting taxes on corporations and the wealthy would trigger large returns as the savings would be re-invested in the economy, in effect paying for the cuts. The Office of Management and Budget debunked this myth with actual analysis, prompting Stockman to confess publicly that "None of us really understands what's going on with all these numbers... the whole thing is premised on faith, on a belief about how the world works."

'Trickle-down' wasn't real economic theory; it was conservative ideology. And when Stockman later said publicly that the tax cuts really were, in fact, a valentine to business, calling the whole thing a 'Trojan horse', he was castigated by the president.

(Forty years later, 'trickle-down' has yet to function as promised, even though the current crop of GOP politicians continue to shop it; the money the uber-wealthy are saving on their tax bills isn't and never has been re-invested in the economy. It sits in off-shore accounts.)

A firestorm of deregulation followed the tax cuts, stagnating the prosperity of the middle class as the growth of the minimum wage dropped away and economic inequality surged. The push for privatization of government began in earnest, sending healthcare costs into the stratosphere, and barriers to the exporting of US manufacturing to nations where labor was far cheaper evaporated. The export of US manufacturing to other countries, gutting the domestic jobs market as it dismantled unions, was accompanied by a breathtaking surge in the trade deficit. Reagan inherited from Carter a deficit of only $13 billion; when he left office, it had soared to a mind-blowing $685 billion.

Perhaps most damning was the elimination of the Fairness Doctrine in 1987. The policy that had protected the integrity of public information since the dawn of radio was dropped, enabling the wild-west, anything-goes parade of disinformation and outright deception that clogs up media today. The airwaves ceased to be conduits for news and became what they are today – ideology pipelines.

Neoliberalism was off and running. The global, regulation-free landscape for the cultivation of wealth envisioned by Friedman and his cohorts was finally taking shape. The transformation of the US government from the middle-class-building, consumer-protecting, civil-rights-promoting agency it had become since the New Deal into capitalism's passive enabler was well underway.

In actual practice, neoliberalism has turned out to be a very ugly thing, even though many of its core goals look good on paper. For instance,

1. Relying on deregulation to achieve global economic parity means reducing the authority of government overall, leading to unrestrained capitalism, inequality, and diminishment of civil rights;
2. Unregulated economies permit corporations to run roughshod over the citizenry, nature, and each other, leading to a destructive winner-take-all landscape that ultimately destroys what it's exploiting;
3. The assumption that the "natural moral order" of humankind is most properly facilitated by market dynamics is naive at best, craven at worst, and in fact unleashes our darkest side;
4. The neoliberal tenet that government's role should be limited to national defense and internal policing, and should have no part in

the well-being of the citizenry, which should be left to the market - well, we've seen how the market handles human well-being.

Again, some of this is well-intentioned; yes, we need a flourishing global economy, and capitalism itself is a source of prosperity and innovation - but unrestrained capitalism and unregulated economy bring out the worst in those who are pulling the levers of the world. We have so many examples of this on the ground in front of us right now, we rapidly lose count.

Democrats are not innocent in this, let's be clear. Bill Clinton, for instance, signed off on the removal of the firewall between commercial and investment banking, in place since the Thirties to prevent another great depression - a major neoliberal win that gifted us with the banking crisis of the mid-2000s. He did this as part of a party agenda to get Democratic politicians closer to business, which was seen as a high priority in the Nineties in the shadow of the Gingrich speakership. Obama was likewise cooperative and compromising where the Right's deregulation agenda was concerned.

Social democracy remains our best option. Yes, let's have free trade, but not completely unregulated trade; let's have regulation, but just what's needed for effective citizen/consumer/environmental protection. And let's emphatically decouple economic regulation from civil rights. Above all, let's have the maintenance of the national and global economies be evidence-based, not subject to the whims and influence of the wealthy. Forty years of Reaganomics have surely established what's good for us and bad for us with great clarity.

Joe Biden took that lesson to heart.

Oligarchy in the 21st Century

"Oligarchs have unsuccessfully tried, twice, to replace democracy in America with oligarchy," wrote Hartmann. "Today, they are nearly finished with not only attempting a third time to change the American experiment from a democracy to an oligarchy, but pushing to then transition our nation from oligarchy to outright tyranny.

"We are living through America's third struggle with oligarchy. It began in 1971, when Lewis Powell, himself a proud agent of the tobacco oligarchs, laid out in a famous memo to the US Chamber of Commerce a plan for the various oligarchs of America to stop competing and organize to take over the US government. By 1980, the plan was in full flower, and by the late 1990s, the oligarchs directly or indirectly controlled a majority of the states, the entire Republican Party, and, at the federal level, well over half of the Democratic Party. By 2005, oligarchic control over the executive branch of our federal government was largely in place, and it was cemented with the Trump administration. When Donald Trump - himself an oligarch - came to power in January 2017, he and his agents embarked on a campaign to destroy the institutions of America that had been so carefully built up over more than 240 years. They succeeded in damaging and corrupting every single federal regulatory agency and turned the foundational departments within the executive branch into full-fledged agents of the Trump oligarchy."

Midway through the 21st century's third decade, that's exactly where we find ourselves.

The oligarchic cycle that began in the Forties, as World War II was drawing to a close, saw the emergence of neoliberalism and its takeover of US politics and economics with the election of Ronald Reagan, is peaking. The latest attempt of the oligarchy to assert its control over the West is coming to its climax.

The slow and steady march of the current oligarchy, personified by the Koch Brothers in the early 21st century and by tech uber-billionaires Elon Musk and Jeff Bezos et al more recently, has resulted in the greatest wealth gap in world history, let alone the US.

It has placed Musk, who sought greater control of social media through his 2023 acquisition of X (neé Twitter) and who has ingratiated himself into a virtual shadow presidency of the US through his pandering to Donald Trump (now reelected), in a position of unprecedented potential dominance.

All of this occurred as a fierce reaction to the presidency of Joe Biden, which represented an overt rejection and refutation of the neoliberalism born of the Walter Lippmann Colloquium and asserted during the Reagan Years. Biden's emphatic goal was to return the United States to that pre-Reagan era of middle class expansion and prosperity that had followed the implementation of the New Deal and the end of World War II.

Historian Heather Cox Richardson summarized the Biden Administration's initiatives and their success, as well as the consequences of Trump's reelection, in an essay published on Nov. 15, 2024:

"President Joe Biden rejected the neoliberalism of the previous 40 years that had moved about $50 trillion dollars from the bottom 90% of Americans to the top 1%. Those embracing that theory maintain that the government should let markets operate without regulation, concentrating wealth among a few people who will invest it more efficiently than they can if the government intervenes with regulations or taxes that hamper the ability of investors to amass wealth.

"Biden and Harris returned the U.S. to the model that both parties had embraced until 1981: the idea that the government should regulate business, provide a basic social safety net, promote infrastructure, and protect civil rights. That system had reduced extremes of wealth in the US after the Great Depression and given most Americans a path to prosperity.

"Biden's policies worked, enabling the US to recover from the pandemic more quickly than any other country with a modern economy, sending unemployment to historic lows, and raising wages faster than inflation for the bottom 80% of Americans.

"Trump and his advisors embrace the neoliberalism Biden rejected. Rather than invest in the economy to create opportunities for middle-class Americans and those just starting out, they want to slash the existing government to free up more capital for investors.

"Trump has tapped the world's richest man, Elon Musk, who invested at least $132 million in cash in Trump's campaign as well as the in-kind gift of the support of X, and former pharmaceutical executive Vivek Ramaswamy to run a 'Department of Government Efficiency', or DOGE, named for Musk's favorite cryptocurrency.

According to the Washington Post's Jeff Stein, Elizabeth Dwoskin, Cat Zakrzewski, and Jacob Bogage, people around Musk say the group is intended to 'apply slash-and-burn business ideologies to the US government.' Musk has vowed to slash 'at least' $2 trillion from the federal budget and has warned it will create 'hardship.'

"That the people embracing this plan see a world in which a few elites run things showed in today's social media post by the 'DOGE.' The post called for 'super high-IQ small-government revolutionaries willing to work 80+ hours per week on unglamorous cost-cutting. If that's you, DM this account. Elon & Vivek will review the top 1% of applicants.'

"Such cuts would be enormously unpopular, and in the *Washington Post* yesterday, Stein, Dwoskin, Zakrzewski, and Bogage reported that Trump's aides are exploring ways to enact dramatic cuts to the government without congressional approval. Key among those is simply refusing to release the money Congress appropriates for programs Musk and Trump want to cut. This is known as 'impoundment,' and Congress made it illegal in 1974 after President Richard Nixon tried to shape the government to his wishes by refusing to fund congressional programs he opposed.

"Trump tried to do this quietly in 2019 by refusing to release the money Congress had appropriated for Ukraine to fund its fight against Russian incursions until Ukraine president Volodymyr Zelensky smeared Biden. When the threat came to light, the House of Representatives impeached Trump. Although the Senate ultimately acquitted Trump, according to

Senator Ted Cruz (R-TX) all the Republican senators agreed he had done as the House charged.

"Now Trump's team apparently hopes that a pliant Supreme Court will declare the 1974 Impoundment Control Act unconstitutional, permitting Trump - or Vice President JD Vance, should Trump not be able to fulfill his term - to shape the government without consulting Congress.

"Because of the 2024 presidential election, Trump will soon be able to return the country to the neoliberal vision of the 40 years before Biden, supercharging it with the help of unelected billionaire Elon Musk, who recently claimed the title of being the 'George Soros of the right,' a reference to the liberal philanthropist who has been the bogeyman of right-wing pundits.

"But it's not at all clear that Americans actually want that supercharged neoliberalism. As vote counts are continuing [after the Nov. 2024 election], it has become clear that Trump's victory was slim indeed. New numbers from Nate Silver suggest he will not clear 50% of voters."

Has oligarchy finally won in the US? Does Biden's defeat, in the face of his David-v.-Goliath challenge to neoliberalism, represent the breaking of Hartmann's cycle of oligarchy, signaling the end of American democracy?

Such a conclusion is premature. While the machinations that led to Trump's victory and Musk's ascendance are certainly of great concern, and concern over Trump's plans to deliberately eradicate most of the infrastructure of the federal government is greater still, the fact is that the policies he plans to implement are as dangerous to the oligarchy as they are to the US citizenry. They will create tremendous instability, and Elon Musk notwithstanding, the oligarchy as a whole eschews instability, and the economic uncertainty and potential upheaval that accompany it. Many of Trump's proposals are likely to fall away, and his slash-and-burn plans are likely to encounter considerable Congressional resistance, even among Republicans.

And there are two additional factors that inspire hope for a return to a pro-middle class economy in the US, if not a truncation of oligarchic power. Following Trump's election, the once-again-Republican Senate elected John Thune to the post of Majority Leader, rejecting Trump's choice (Rick Scott). This assertion of independence in the Senate foreshadows resistance to Trump, as the pro-business faction of Senate Republicans is as wary of economic and international instability – all of which Trump embodies – as the oligarchy itself is.

Finally, there is traditionally a midterm pushback against new administrations, and the one coming in 2026 is likely to be a doozy after the wake-up call of Trump's reelection and the almost certain economic and international turmoil that will occur in the interim. The Republican Senate is already poised to resist Trump, and a 2027 Democratic Congress most certainly will.

Pushing back against Trump and Elon Musk, however, does not represent a return to Biden's anti-neoliberalism path for the country, nor does it do anything to unseat the oligarchy that is now asserting itself. It does, however, draw the battle lines more clearly for those who didn't fully understand what was going on during Biden presidency, aren't really aware of what the oligarchy is and what it seeks (Musk will clarify it tremendously), and haven't been paying enough attention to the economic big picture in the United States.

Two years from now, those lines will be more clear. What kind of nation America really wants to be will become clearer still.

Oligarchy 2024:
Donald Trump and Elon Musk

Perhaps the most prominent marker of Oligarchy's control of the federal government is the emerging partnership between President-elect Donald Trump and Elon Musk, the richest man in the world.

Musk backed Trump and other Republicans in the 2024 election to the tune of $277 million. The returning president's "thank you" to Musk will be to appoint him to lead a new government spending review panel, the Department of Government Efficiency, alongside fellow oligarch Vivek Ramaswamy. Between them, they have publicly declared that they will "gut the federal government," in Musk's words, slashing budgets and regulations without mercy - $2 trillions worth. He also made clear that Social Security and Medicare will not be spared.

Besides Social Security and Medicare, the DOGE is targeting the following for elimination or drastic reduction:

- The Department of Education
- The Department of Defense (elimination of key

programs)

- The Consumer Financial Protection Bureau
- The Internal Revenue Service

The partnership between Trump and Musk is surely one of convenience. It is hard to imagine that either man truly admires the other, and underneath their stated intentions they have radically different agendas. The fact is that Musk's fortune is 100 times greater than Trump's, and he stands to gain far more through deregulation and tax breaks.

The impact of their partnership on public perception is central to any understanding of the actions they have planned and the consequences. They are leveraging their status as billionaires in pursuit of an agenda that neither truly has the knowledge or experience to meaningfully execute. Put another way, they want to look good gutting the government; no one should believe they have the knowledge to actually pursue it judiciously.

Yet this is textbook Oligarchy: the Oligarch believes, based solely on his possession of great wealth, that he is inherently better equipped to decide for everyone else how society should work. There are considerable impediments that mercifully stand before them, so the degree to which DOGE can proceed is unclear; but the damage that can be wrought on the US and global economy, to say nothing of the damage to the lives of ordinary Americans, cannot be overstated.

"These men are very wealthy and very powerful, but government is more wealthy and powerful. Elon Musk is a billionaire, but government is a trillionaire," wrote Gil Duran of George Lakoff's FrameLab. "Governments can fight wars; Elon Musk can't. Government can put you behind bars for your crimes; Elon Musk can't do that. Not yet, right? If they can destroy the power of the state, then that power will be in their hands. Right now, they see rules and laws as a threat. Supposedly, they're libertarians, so that means you'd want to eliminate these regulations and laws for everybody and do what thou wilt shall be the whole of the law."

We'll see.

Oligarchy:
What to Do About It

It's not just a matter of preserving democracy against the Oligarchy's efforts to overthrow it. The Oligarchy is in place; in addition to defending democracy, we need to remove the Oligarchy from its current political perch.

Gilens and Page, who performed the study above establishing the Oligarchy's control of the federal government, suggest that several steps are crucial in bringing this about. Gilens has said that "meaningful campaign finance reform is the single, most promising avenue" for dislodging the Oligarchy.

Others, they said, include the implementation of ranked choice voting and open primaries, to strengthen the voice of the electorate through the dilution of the current two-party duopoly.

Hartmann points out that the Oligarchy's current entrenchment results from several key activities:

"In every case, the process followed the path that America has been on since the Powell Memo and the Reagan Revolution:

- Oligarchs fund media, lobbyists, and think tanks that seize the public dialogue while burrowing deeply into popular media and

academia.
- They use the power of that money to further weaken laws keeping money out of politics.
- They move from ownership of individual politicians to ownership of an entire political party.
- They use that party to seize control of government itself and then "deconstruct the administrative state."
- Without the state protecting the people, and with the state controlling elections in a way that widely disenfranchises the victims of the oligarchy, democracy becomes a sham exercise and a police state emerges to enforce the new economic and social order."

He lists a number of actions that can be taken to undo these steps:

- **End the Oligarch's media empire.** Breaking up Murdoch media would be a strong step forward.
- **Strengthen the free press.** "America needs to recognize not just journalists but acts of journalism, regardless of who commits them."
- **Provide economic rights for all.** In addition to the political rights enumerated by the Constitution, we should codify economic rights in the US – the right to employment, housing, healthcare, education, and freedom from

economic hardship. Currently, these are privileges, not rights (they are rights in every other advanced Western nation).

- **Tax the rich again.** "It's time to return to the rational tax policy that helped [Eisenhower] build new infrastructure all across our nation while presiding over a strong, prosperous economy."
- **Prosecute election cheaters.** "Of all the various crimes against our republic committed by the Trump Administration, this is the most serious, because the most common way that autocrats and tyrants hold power forever once they've gained it is by politicizing the agencies of government."
- **Have publicly-funded elections.** "The lifeblood of Oligarchy is the ability to use money to influence politics. Only when big money is torn out of politics will the Oligarchs be defeated."
- **Resist!** "As tyranny stretches out its putrid, rotting arm across America, support those who stand in its way. Better, join them!"
- **Maintain election integrity.** "Most oligarchies preserve many of the trappings of democracy to give them legitimacy... it's pretty much the same here in the United States, and if things don't change, the window during which contemporary oligarchs can be overthrown will

pass."

- **Build progressive organizations.** The Oligarchy and the neoliberal GOP have been building supporting institutions for decades, while the Democrats have been putting all their resources into boots-on-the-ground problem-fixing. The Democrats must start building out infrastructure for long-term initiatives to win hearts and minds and work on better policy offerings.
- **Help the Republican GOP rebuild.** The GOP used to be in alignment with the Democrats on most matters of public policy; that changed with Reagan and the neoliberal agenda, and needs to change back. "Opposition parties are good things; they help clarify and sharpen issues for voters and in policy debate. Reach out to your GOP friends who aren't total racists or misogynists and help them bring their party back to its pre-Reagan rationality."
- Rebuild the Democratic Party. The Democrats are no prize themselves these days, Hartmann wrote. "The most effective way to use politics to block oligarchy in America is not to wait for some billionaire to run a bunch of ads on TV or exhort people to vote. It's to build strong and resilient democratic institutions, from school boards to town councils to the Democratic Party itself. And that requires us to show up

and participate."

Not everyone can do all of these things; but everyone can do some of these things. Pick some and get to work!

While there's still time.

Afterword:
Empathy, Capitalism, and the Oligarch

Empathy is hard-wired into the human brain. It is a survival mechanism that is very rare in the animal kingdom in general, and uncommon even in higher mammals. It isn't a choice, it isn't a learned thing; it is built in - we roll off the factory floor with it.

That said, the amount of empathy experienced by any one individual often differs somewhat from that of any other; there is variability in how much empathy each of us feels.

More than that, it's not all about how much empathy we feel; it's as much about how much - and in what ways - society trains us to express it. Here, too, there is considerable variability.

Gary Olson addresses this in his excellent book *Empathy Imperiled: Capitalism, Culture, and the Brain*. His premise is that capitalism, by design, suppresses our natural hard-wired imperative to work together to survive. Empathy is the engine of cooperation, and we have used that engine to travel very far very quickly, in evolutionary terms.

Capitalism does damage in this domain on several levels, Olson asserts. To begin with, it is based on a set of presuppositions that are increasingly odds with the findings of neurophysiology, evolutionary anthropology and behavioral genetics: it assumes that human beings are naturally selfish, that our deep impulse is not cooperation but competition.

Here, Olson has a mountain to climb, for it is certainly true that we are immersed in examples of human selfishness daily, that we have all committed acts of selfishness at one time or another, and that selfishness is certainly the rule among many species other than our own. But he has the latest research on his side: the deeper we dive into our paleolithic roots, the clearer it becomes that cooperation, not competition, kept us alive through hundreds of thousands of years under predation. Moreover, the more we learn about the wiring of the human brain, the more we see 'cooperation circuits', rather than 'competition circuits'.

The disconnect, Olson demonstrates, is in the social structures we are born and raised in - capitalism being the most destructive of the lot. The background messages of capitalism, firmly perpetuated by the oligarchy, are that we are all in competition with one another, that our personal mission is acquisition and that the ideal position in society is one of dominance. Moreover, he articulates, the member wishing to thrive must constantly be on guard, wary of others, alert for the possibility of deceit and exploitation, and reluctant to share.

These ideas, per Olson, are not innate but unnatural, created by the oligarchic few to manipulate the many, and that capitalism as an expression of human nature is not only not constructive but toxic.

He quotes Joel Bakan: "As the corporation comes to dominate society - through, among other things, privatization and commercialization -□its□ideal conception of human nature becomes dominant, too. And it is a frightening prospect. The corporation, after all, is deliberately designed to be a psychopath: purely self-interested, incapable of concern for others, amoral and without conscience - in a word, inhuman - and its goal... is to ensure that the human beings who it is interacting with, you and me, also become inhuman."

There is, to be sure, nothing of the natural human to be found in the corporate citizen – and, by extension, the oligarchy - who operate according to rules that fly in the face of natural human cooperation. They have more in common with the leopard and wolf, whose concerns never extend beyond self, and whose only goal is to feed. There is nothing of the communities of the veldt, whose members lived and loved and died as one, mastering the harshest of worlds with new ways, thriving and moving forward at astonishing pace through the simple mechanism of sharing everything with everyone.

All of that said, it is certainly true that not all competition is unhealthy, not all business bloodthirsty; that the act of negotiation is often the best mode of cooperation; that motivations matter. But gone are the days, Olson argues, when oligarchs could claim the high ground in the march of social progress, or any ownership at all of the human profile. On the data, on the history, on the examples emerging around us, the lie is put to the textbook distortions of Adam Smith: the Invisible Hand, we are rediscovering, exists not to push, but to reach out...

Series Afterword:
Preserving Democracy

That democracy in the United States – and throughout the Western world, really – is on the ropes is painfully obvious to anyone who turns on the news. Authoritarianism is on the march, and the Christian Nationalists are only one of several groups that seeks to bring democracy down and install autocracy in its place.

What can be done about this?

At the institutional level, much can be done and is being done: political parties adhering to the traditional principles of democracy are learning from their mistakes and rethinking their strategies and tactics; the Constitutional guardrails of democracy in the US remain in place, at least for now, and there are thousands of public servants doing all they can to keep them there.

But what can the individual do?

Fortunately, we have European neighbors who have been here before, all too often: dealing with authoritarian regimes that have ripped democracy away from them and left them powerless. And they have shared their to-do lists with us, in this case by way of Martin Mycielski, Director of Public Affairs of the Open Dialog Foundation in Brussels:

- They will claim their ascendance represents the 'will of the people,' rather than the manipulative victory of a minority; that victory gives them no right to cross legal boundaries.

- They took power through unified alliance. That power will only be returned to the people if they, too, are unified. Pursue that unity!
- They have made strong strategic use of manipulated media; push back hard in support of legitimate news sources and the autonomy of journalists.
- Commit to critical thinking, practice is assiduously, and encourage others to do the same.
- They will distract, distract, distract, in order to obfuscate their real agenda. Look through the noise and chaos at what's really happening, and point it out to others.
- They will attack and injure what matters most, to maintain that distraction. It will be painful to watch. Don't let it pull your attention away from reclaiming democracy.
- Oppose any proposed laws that limit the freedom of citizens to freely assemble.
- Don't let them control the framing of public discourse. For decades, they have skillfully (even artfully) manipulated public debate with carefully targeted language. Don't adopt their frames – learn as much as you can about framing (from George Lakoff, for one) and work to reframe the debate.
- Teach the children in your life the real history of your country, and make sure they learn to think critically as well.

Mycielski goes on to call for more personal investment – attitude adjustment, if we will, for those who are willing to hold out for the recovery of democracy:

- Resist indifference
- Eschew fear, and embolden others to, as well
- Organize; find allies and create strong bonds
- Resist efforts to divide; remain civil and open, even to ideological opponents
- Learn from the mistakes that brought us to this point, and know what to do differently next time
- Persevere

Historian and Andrew Carnegie Fellow Timothy Snyder, author of *On Tyranny* and *On Freedom*, offers his own personal to-do list:

- *Don't "obey in advance"*. "Most of the power of authoritarianism is freely given."
- *Defend institutions*. "It is institutions that help us to preserve democracy."
- *Take responsibility for the face of the world.* Resist the adoption of symbols that separate us.
- *Believe in truth*. "To abandon facts is to abandon freedom."
- *Investigate*. "Figure things out for yourself. Spend more time with long articles... Take responsibility for what you communicate to others."

- *Make eye contact and small talk.* "It is a way to stay in touch with your surroundings, break down social barriers, and understand whom you should and should not trust."
- *Practice corporeal politics.* Get out into the world. "Put your body in unfamiliar places with unfamiliar people. Make new friends and march with them."
- *Guard your privacy.* "Scrub your computer of malware. Remember that email is skywriting. Have personal exchanges in person."
- *Learn from peers in other countries.* As with Mycielski above, understand that friendships abroad can inform us; "No country is going to find a solution by itself."
- *Be calm when the unthinkable arrives.* "Modern tyranny is terror management. Do not fall for it."
- *Be a patriot.* "Set a good example of what America means for the generations to come."
- *Be courageous.* "If none of us is prepared to die for freedom, then all of us will die under tyranny."

Bibliography/
Recommended Reading

Capitalism as Oligarchy, Jim O'Reilly. JOR, 2015.

Empathy Imperiled: Capitalism, Culture, and the Brain, Gary Olson. Springer, 2012.

The Hidden History of American Democracy, Thom Hartmann. Berrett-Koehler Publishers, 2023.

The Hidden History of American Oligarchy, Thom Hartmann. Berrett-Koehler Publishers, 2021.

John Adams and the Fear of American Oligarchy, Luke Mayville. Princeton University Press, 2016.

Oligarchy, Jeffrey A. Winters. Cambridge University Press, 2011.

Revolt of the Rich, David N. Gibbs. Columbia University Press, 2024.

https://www.carnegie.org/our-work/article/twenty-lessons-fighting-tyranny/

https://verfassungsblog.de/the-authoritarian-regime-survival-guide/

About the Author

Scott Robinson is an AI technologist, social scientist, public speaker and musician, and serves as Director of Technology and Content for the non-profit Humanity Prime.

He can be found at

scott.robinson@glenmillscience.com